navigating
minefields

A YOUNG MAN'S BLUEPRINT FOR SUCCESS
ON LIFE'S BATTLEFIELD

VICTORIA DUERSTOCK
AND BETHANY JETT

END GAME
Press

End Game Press books may be purchased in bulk at special discounts for sales promotion, corporate gifts, ministry, fund-raising, or educational purposes. Special editions can also be created to specifications. For details, contact Special Sales Dept., End Game Press, P.O. Box 206, Nesbit, MS 38651 or info@endgamepress.com.

Visit our website at www.endgamepress.com.

Published in association with Cyle Young of the Cyle Young Literary Elite, LLC

Library of Congress Control Number: 2021940033
ISBN: 978-1-63797-004-1
eBook ISBN: 978-1-63797-005-8

Quote page 165 from https://timchavel.blogspot.com/2008/02/gary-smalley. html?m=1. Quote page 31 from https://www.goodreads.com/author/ quotes/12008.Peter_F_Drucker. Quote page 123 from https://www.forbes.com/ sites/kevinkruse/2012/10/16/quotes-on-leadership/?sh=34b41de22feb. Quote page 195 from https://wisdomquotes.com/inspirational-quotes-for-men/.

Cover Design by Greg Jackson, Thinkpen Design
Interior design by Marisa Jackson for TLC Book Design, TLCBookDesign.com.

Printed in India
RRD
10 9 8 7 6 5 4 3 2 1

This book is dedicated to my three incredible sons—Jeremy, Jedidiah, and Josiah and to every young man who wants to make something of his life.

BETHANY JETT

There are so many words left unsaid in the course of a mother's days. While not all-inclusive, *Navigating Minefields* contains much of the encouragement I wish to share with my own son, Connor. I dedicate this book to him and other boys just like him who are rapidly becoming men.

VICTORIA DUERSTOCK

table of contents

INTRODUCTION

You probably didn't buy this book.

If you saw it on a shelf, you may have picked it up, assuming it had something to do with video games or cheat codes ... only to be disappointed to find that it's a book written by moms.

After all, who wants to read a series of ~~lectures~~ essays that they've heard day in and day out?

Someone probably put this book in your hands because they wanted to make sure you had access to the advice you'll need to make it through life. Sometimes it's easier to pick up a book than to make a phone call, so here it is. We've compiled in this book all the advice we moms teach our sons and want them to have access to when they're away from home, making tough choices and real-world decisions.

Too many adults never learn these lessons, and sometimes it's no fault of their own. Maybe there wasn't someone who could teach them, or perhaps no one shoved a book like this into their hands.

You are capable of doing amazing things. Even if you think that you've messed up, or if you haven't figured out what your talents and skills are yet, that's okay. Rest assured: There is a plan for you, and the advice in this book will help you make the best decisions you can in every area of your life.

CHAPTER 1

On Controlling Your Anger

You are not the Hulk.

When someone gets under your skin, the best thing you can do is to rise above—but trust me, I know it is much easier said than done.

Rarely does losing your temper bring you what you want. If you can learn this simple but difficult lesson early in life, it will move mountains for you. Respond to a situation instead of reacting to it and you'll lock in a reputation for having the ability to lead through adversity.

> "Nonviolence means avoiding not only external physical violence, but also

> internal violence of spirit. You not only refuse
> to shoot a man, but you refuse to hate him."[1]
>
> MARTIN LUTHER KING, JR.

The overflow of our heart is what pours out through our lives and is reflected in our decisions, speech, and even in the way we treat others.

Violence brings upon more violence and lies develop into more lies. This is an internal struggle, and it really comes down to being a heart issue.

Many times, when someone lashes out aggressively, it is a reaction to the violence they have experienced themselves. Other times, it's a defense mechanism spurred on by insecurity.

It begs the question, "Is it ever okay to be violent?"

There is perhaps one exception. Defense. You fight to protect yourself, your family, and your country. That's it.

We shouldn't mess with people just to make them mad.

Antagonizing someone is pointless because, truly, what does it accomplish? Sometimes the best way we can treat people is to leave them alone and avoid provoking, especially when they're not doing anything to you in the first place.

Consider Bruce Banner, the Hulk's alter ego. When someone would upset him, he had to control his anger so his secret wouldn't get out. If we met the "Green Goliath" in real life, we wouldn't want to push him too far. And we shouldn't want to push other people's buttons either.

Don't say something just to get a rise out of someone or play a joke that will be hurtful or embarrassing. You can avoid situations where violence could erupt by treating others with respect. And when someone makes you angry, take a few deep breaths, maintain your composure, and leave the Hulk-smashes for the big screen.

CHAPTER **2**

blow up or
slow down

You've probably noticed by now how easy it is to get upset. Anger can well up in the heat of the moment, or for practically no reason at all. The surge of hormones in young manhood can make the best boys suddenly difficult and cause relationships to be strained because of the mighty mood swings.

Learning not to blow up over the slightest irritation is a sign of maturity. Responding to friends and even family members in an appropriate and measured way instead of in anger is often a challenge. When others don't respect your space, your things, or your time, it can be easy to give them a piece of your mind. Unfortunately, the effort to have others respect your boundaries often veers into unkindness

9

and mean-spiritedness. This keeps you from staying on task while asking others to respect your wishes.

Being slow to anger takes practice. Just like many other things we will discuss in this book, it's not a one-and-done type of thing. Instead, you will likely fail, need to ask for forgiveness, and need to work hard to do better next time. Everyone needs to practice self-control, and it really is practice. It doesn't come easily.

If you fail, don't stop trying. Keep getting back up and work to become better. Over time, and through much practice, we all can develop the habit of being slow to anger.

> "Anger is an acid that can do more harm to the vessel in which it is stored than to anything on which it is poured."[2]
>
> MARK TWAIN

CHAPTER 3

watch your response

ver notice how quickly arguments escalate? I mean escalate like from zero to a hundred in a Ferrari on an open highway. Arguments can fly quick. Do you have a short fuse? A quick trigger? Do you fly off the handle for practically no reason at all?

If so, here's what I recommend:

Slow your response time.

Don't respond immediately.

Bite your tongue if you must.

Just remember that a soft response, a quiet manner of speaking, can dump a whole lot of water on a fire that might otherwise burn out of control, harming everyone in its path.

Diffusing an argument isn't easy, especially if you believe you are right and the other person is wrong. But when it comes to relationships, we must learn the value in not needing to prove our point. Would you rather live in harmony and peace with others around you, or would you rather be right? If we don't want to argue all the time with our loved ones, then we must choose to simply let some things go.

While it may not always be an easy task, or even possible, try to make it a habit to *think* before you *speak*. To *think* requires that we stop and listen to what's actually being said versus what we think the other person is saying. It involves trying to understand the other person's perspective.

This is an important part of growing up.

> "I'm generally slow to anger, quick to forgive, and I take in information before making decisions. So no matter how controversial the decision, my general demeanour is to put on a white lab coat and gloves and look at the evidence, weigh the arguments and see what makes sense."[3]
>
> PETER BLAIR HENRY

what you do
has far bigger
impact than
what you say.

STEPHEN COVEY

how to apologize and defuse the argument

When you do something wrong, the best thing to do is take responsibility. I can't tell you how many adults have never harnessed the power that lives inside of these simple phrases:

I'm sorry.

Please forgive me.

How can I make it up to you?

Those three sentences can shift a situation out of the blame game and instead both parties can become solution oriented. Instead of pointing fingers at others, let's learn to point the finger at *ourselves*.

Assuming we haven't seriously hurt anyone or committed a felony, usually a heartfelt apology—accompanied with an offer to make amends—is enough to defuse the situation. Sadly, though, many people consider an apology to be a sign of weakness when instead it is actually a sign of strength.

> "Apologizing does not always mean that you are wrong and the other person is right. It just means that you value your relationship more than your ego."[4]
>
> MARK MATTHEWS

The behaviors that follow an apology will provide the evidence you need to know whether the person was sincere. When we're sorry for something we've done, we stop the behavior. It's that action that supports the apology.

Taking responsibility for our actions can keep the argument from escalating; in the process, we prevent ourselves from doing or saying something that we will need to apologize for in the future.

Please note: If someone hurts you and then apologizes, but then that person continues to hurt you, it's likely that the apology is not coming from a genuine place. It's best, in those situations, to immediately confide in someone you can trust. Not sure who can help you? Check out the list of free 24/7 hotline numbers found in the back of this book.

on tearing down

It might seem a bit odd to talk about gossip as we talk to you young men; but sadly, gossip has become almost a way of life in today's culture. Talking behind someone's back has become completely acceptable—especially if that person is outside of your circle. Sometimes what begins as a conversation centered on sharing information transitions into trash-talking someone. Be careful! If the information you're sharing is not helpful or kind, it's probably best to remain quiet.

Can I let you in on something too? If you have a friend who constantly talks about others and their secrets, you can bet your last dollar that they will do (or already have done) the same concerning you and your secrets.

> **"Isn't it kind of silly to think that tearing someone else down builds you up?"**[5]
>
> SEAN COVEY

How do I know this? Because that person obviously has a pattern of gossip in their life. If that's the case, then you can't trust that their friendship will be genuine. The kind of person who actively tries to take other people down is self-focused and will never care about you like a real friend should.

Sometimes it's easy to gossip because it builds status with others. When we share the tidbits of information we know about a person, it sometimes makes it seem like we are *someone special.* We gain some sort of brownie points in our friendships ... except that we don't. The little bit of gossip that we shared with a friend may have just started as a spark, but when that friend shares it with others, that spark soon grows into a wildfire.

Watch out!

Gossip kills friendships.

It ruins reputations.

It hurts people.

I challenge you to be the kind of young man who is willing to avoid participating in these gossip games.

Dare to be different. Stand apart from the crowd.

a lazy life

aziness is hard to fight. The temptation occurs naturally, and it's difficult to remove. But the fruit of a lazy life is poverty, disappointment, and discouragement. A lazy life is the easiest thing for someone to accomplish. Why? Because it doesn't take any work to be lazy. Just avoid all responsibility and hide when it's time to work!

Laziness comes in all all sorts of shapes and sizes. You might choose to spend your time lying in bed, or on the sofa binge-watching Netflix, or playing forty-two rounds of Fortnight. Whatever it looks like in your life, laziness feels pretty good for the time being. Am I right? A habit of laziness doesn't take long to establish, and it is an incredibly difficult habit to break.

Unfortunately, the habits you're building now can guide you throughout the rest of your life.

Contrary to popular opinion, a lazy life is far from a good life.

> "Laziness travels so slowly that poverty soon overtakes him."[6]
>
> BENJAMIN FRANKLIN

On the other hand, the diligent person is ready to serve and to be helpful when and where he is needed. The person who lends a hand to others in need, who works even when he doesn't feel like it, will avoid a life of desperation. A life of thriving instead of just surviving is reserved for someone who refuses to take the easy road of laziness.

When you choose to be diligent in work, it gets noticed.

The act of being exceptional doesn't take as much effort as it used to.

Show up, be early, work hard, look people in the eyes, speak clearly, and *refuse to be lazy*.

Trust me when I say that you will excel in this life if you choose to be a diligent worker!

inspiration, not manipulation

No one teaches us how to become a master manipulator. We seem to have picked up this character trait all on our own.

Manipulating a situation, or a person, involves adjusting circumstances or utilizing emotions in an effort to control an outcome. The art (if you can call it that) of manipulation is knowing the person you're trying to manipulate, and then using guilt or fear as a means of power.

> **"If we inspire people, they will give us more than we asked for.**

> **If we manipulate them, they will give us exactly what we paid for."[7]**
>
> SIMON SINEK, popular thought leader and bestselling author of *Start with Why*

There is a fine line between inspiration and manipulation, and often it's the *motivation* that can help determine which side of the fence we're on. When we inspire people, the idea is that we arm them with the tools they need to go forth and conquer. There is not a kickback for us involved.

Manipulating someone usually means that we're going to get something out of the arrangement. There is a goal in mind, and we need to use someone else to attain the goal—whether that person is aware of the ultimate endgame, or not.

When we inspire people, we allow them to catch the vision. We give them space to think and act in their own way and on their own timetable.

When we manipulate, however, we have to maintain an element of control. This often leads to a punishment for anyone who doesn't fall in line.

Here are some warning signs that someone might be manipulating *you*:

1. You feel like you can't say *no*.
2. Access to certain (or all) friends or family members is restricted or discouraged.
3. Conversations include the phrase "If you really loved me" or "If you were really my friend."
4. You feel responsible for the other person's emotional state. If they get mad or violent, it's because of something *you* did or didn't do. It never seems to be their own fault.
5. Violence or Abuse. If this is the case, seek help immediately.

If you find yourself nodding along to any of those warning signs, it's time to take a step back and reevaluate that relationship. If you are, in fact, in any type of danger—or if you need help getting out of a bad situation—there are free and anonymous hotlines you can call or text. You can use these hotlines even if it's just to receive a third-party perspective on your situation.

Also, if you find yourself being the manipulator, make the decision to change. Give people the freedom they need to make their own decisions. Allowing people to grow with no strings attached builds the loyalty you're seeking, and it will push you farther down your path to success.

CHAPTER 2

prepare for temptation

We all face temptation. No matter our age or gender, temptation affects each and every one of us. Temptation to lie, steal, and cheat—none of us are immune. Thankfully, we can have self-control that can help us to avoid temptation.

> "Every moment of resistance to temptation is a victory."[8]
>
> FREDERICK WILLIAM FABER

For some reason, the idea of resisting temptation is almost a foreign concept today. Did you know that we actually have a choice in how we respond to temptation? But it seems to be a common opinion that falling for a temptation is inevitable. Like we don't have a chance because we are hardwired to being too weak to resist.

WRONG!

You are absolutely capable of resisting temptation; however, you must do a few things.

You need to prepare.

Prepare to face temptation.

Prepare to avoid temptation.

Prepare to establish boundaries for what you allow yourself to see, hear, and do. Try to avoid people who can tempt you and places that can cause problems.

Don't be fooled into thinking you have no control over what happens to you. No, you don't have to go along with what's going on around you. You will always have the ability to simply say *no*.

Here's what I know to be true: The more often you say *no* and resist temptation, the quicker you will build the habit. And the stronger the habit, the easier it will be to resist when temptation comes searching for you.

lust kills
love's potential

You have easy access today to all manner of disgusting, vile pornographic images. Whether it's on shows and movies, or singers and influencers on YouTube channels, you have unlimited resources for satisfying lust with a tap of a button.

> "The more we are filled with thoughts of lust the less we find true romantic love."[9]
>
> DOUGLAS HORTON

The problem in our society is that so much of what you see portrayed on these screens is false. There is no romantic love or real relationship portrayed in any of it. Mostly it's meant for shock value and to keep people talking about them and watching to see what happens next. Pornography is degrading and demeaning and is not something that young men should have unfettered access to.

And yet, you do.

But just because you have access to it doesn't mean you have to see it, listen to it, or engage with it. You can choose to simply turn it off—or, if you find yourself being unable to look away, consider installing a blocker, a program that will prevent nasty websites from being opened. There are plenty of options out there. If you need that kind of support, it is far better to set boundaries for yourself than to develop an out-of-control addiction.

A mature person will decide to act in this way and set boundaries, especially with the content he consumes.

Your future relationships will be affected by the choices you make today, so I hope you will choose wisely and protect your future by escaping lust in all its forms.

unless
commitment
is made,
there are only
promises and hopes;
but no plans.

PETER F. DRUCKER

CHAPTER 10

skip the sex ... for now

ociety has different rules for boys than they do for girls regarding sex. There's a twisted sense of masculinity that comes with being able to sleep with lots of people, but it's a false cloud of clout or power. Sadly, holding onto your virginity or waiting until you're married to have sex is seen as *weird* for guys—but let's be clear: Sex is too important to just give away.

Abstinence, or waiting for marriage to have sex, isn't always based on religious principles.

What isn't being widely talked about is what sex does emotionally for a guy. Talking and sharing about one's feelings isn't something that comes very easily for a large number of men.

> "Sex is essentially deep. We become what we do with our bodies, and there is no deeper act than sex."[10]
>
> DIETRICH VON HILDEBRAND, philosopher

So … we'll skip any fluffy feeling *mumbo-jumbo* and get straight to the point: Sex is never just sex. There are invisible ties and strings to everyone you sleep with. How far you repress those feelings is up to you.

That said, sex isn't something to use as an emotional weapon. You don't *deserve* it, she doesn't *owe* you, and it's not the ultimate test of true love. While the concept of waiting to have sex until you're married may sound archaic, it's about protection in three areas: physically, emotionally, and relationally.

Protect your body. STDs are rampant, even ones that are transmitted while using a condom, (like HPV).

Protect your heart. Sex is physical, but it's also as intimate as you can get with another person. It develops an emotional bond. Don't diminish the powerful tie it creates.

Protect your future spouse. The ghosts of those who share your bed show up in the marriage in the form of comparison. *Am I as good in bed as* xyz? *Did I do the right things?*

But what if it's "too late" and your virginity is no longer something you can give to your future spouse?

It's never too late.

One of the most loving things you can do is to respect yourself, and *her*, enough to choose to wait from this point forward.

CHAPTER 11

dating dangers

t's time for some plain conversations, and I hope you understand a mother's heart here. It's not that there will never be girls who are good enough for you, but we definitely don't want you to settle. And we want you to be aware that, in this life, the choices you make in dating, engagement, and eventually marriage will affect the trajectory of your life.

This might sound terribly dramatic but hear me out: The girl you will choose to have in your life, long term, is a lifetime of commitment. Make sure that the girl you date isn't constantly trying to change you! Don't get me wrong; I'm all about finding someone who can elevate you into a better person. But be careful. If a girl is always trying to mold your personality or any aspect of yourself—even your sense of style—these are warning signs that she may be controlling.

> **"Don't settle for a relationship that won't let you be yourself."**[11]
> OPRAH

When dating, try to find a girl who shares the same values as you. She should be kind and treat others with respect. Keep in mind that she will most likely reveal only the best aspects of herself to you while you're first dating. There is probably much more you will uncover about her over time.

If she's accustomed to a very privileged lifestyle, be aware of her expectations.

Observe the way she treats her parents, younger siblings, cousins, and even strangers. This will be an indication of how she will treat *your* parents, siblings, and future children.

Why am I warning you of this now? Because, if you date someone for a long time, it will be much more difficult to make a break later. It hurts far worse to say goodbye after you have made an emotional investment, and I want to protect your heart. You want to find a girl to date long term who will be pleasant to be with for a long time! At the same time, you will also need to be the kind of man who will make a great partner in life as well. You need to be someone who is kind, understanding, and caring. You won't regret being that kind of man!

CHAPTER 12

choose the right mate

don't marry a girl who thinks she's a princess. Find a girl who is concerned about putting others first, and then you can treat her like the princess she is.

A princess can turn into a diva *reeeeal* quick, and trust me, that's no fun for anyone.

Trust the people in your life who love you and who have your best interests at heart. They can offer guidance when it comes time to choose your future mate. When someone is in a relationship—especially if they are head-over-heels in love with the person—their common sense can become murky. It can be difficult to see the relationship from an objective standpoint; thus, oh-so-easy-to-dismiss potential warning signs can be missed.

> "Don't let feeling lonely push you into the arms of a person who will make you miserable."[12]
>
> STEPHAN LABOSSIERE (aka @StephanSpeaks), certified relationship coach

Aaaaaaaaa-men.

While there is a healthy level of disagreement in relationships, full-blown shouting arguments should be extremely rare, not the norm.

Yes, it's normal to feel a little jealous at times. Especially when you love someone. But what *isn't* normal is when that jealousy transforms into paranoia.

The right person will want to make you a priority without making you the *only* priority. Find a girl who has goals, dreams, and the hustle and grit to chase them.

When you're in a relationship, there is a certain level of defensiveness that naturally comes with the territory. You love (or *super really like*) this person, and you want your family to like and approve of them as well.

And if you ever hear yourself saying the words "But you don't understand," or "Our relationship is *different*," that is a clear sign that something not quite right might be going on behind the scenes.

Being in love is wonderful, so use wisdom, and not just your emotions, when choosing your future bride.

eat the frog

One of the challenges we face as we navigate adulthood is knowing how to deal with priorities—figuring out what is the most important thing for us to do on a day, and then doing it. Many times, we can find ourselves working through our days with *reactions* instead of *intentions*. For example, when faced with the choice between a project deadline for school, a chore, or games to play, it's easy to choose the game simply because we WANT to.

The reality is that we must set priorities in order to reap the benefits of finishing the job. And if we don't plan ahead, then we could be forever stressed dealing with the results of our procrastination.

I like to encourage young people to eat your peas *before* your dessert.

Mark Twain is known for saying,

> **"If it's your job to eat a frog, it's best to do it first thing in the morning. And if it's your job to eat two frogs, it's best to eat the biggest one first."**[13]

I never liked peas—still don't. And I don't think I'd like to eat frogs either. I'd much rather have a volcano cake, brownie, or chocolate chip cookie. I'm not too discriminating. But if I only ate what I *wanted*, I'd never get around to eating what my body *needs*.

If I start my day by doing only the things I enjoy, then I never do the things I don't.

I have found through the years that a bit of an adjustment on this can also be made that is still beneficial. I negotiate with myself. Maybe you can try this too. I make a deal with myself that sounds like this: *If I spend fifteen minutes on the project I dread, then I can take fifteen minutes to reward myself by doing something fun.* There's nothing magical about fifteen-minute chunks of time. Those amounts can change. But I do try to make them equal swaps.

This gives me the motivation I need to get those challenging tasks out of the way. It's super easy to grab your phone and set a timer on these days too!

if it's a priority
you'll find a way.
if it isn't,
you'll find an excuse.

JIM ROHN

success habits

Self-care is not often regarded as a masculine concept. But if you listen to any CEO or millionaire discuss their morning routines, you will discover that exercise, health, and mental wellness are typically a top priority.

Let's start with the space you occupy. Whether you share a room or have one to yourself, examine the space that is yours. How clean is it? Would you be embarrassed if someone you admired hung out in your bedroom in the condition it's in now? There's a difference between being messy and being dirty.

Clutter is one thing. Filth is another.

Moving on to personal hygiene, do you stay well groomed? Is your hair clean? Are showers a regular part of your daily routine? How about flossing?

According to Business Insider,[15] 76 percent of the rich exercise a minimum of thirty minutes per day. The benefits that exercise provides both body and mind can help us maintain optimum performance in every area of our lives.

A douse of body spray does not cover a multitude of hormonal puberty, stinky-boy smell. Once you get known for being the dirty kid, or the stinky kid, it's a hard reputation to get rid of. A daily shower, plus a coat of deodorant, will keep you from having to worry if the odor is coming from you.

Another habit to incorporate into your routine is reading. If you prefer watching the film over reading the novel, that's okay, but you can still learn to love to read. There are multitudes of books that have yet to make it to the big screen. Don't miss out on them!

In fact, when you listen to interviews with millionaires and billionaires, reading is one of their nonnegotiable habits.

> "I read two hours every day. This habit is responsible for the majority of my success. I don't know many rich people who don't read a lot, but every poor person I know has an X-Box."[16]
>
> BRANDON CARTER, fitness expert and celebrity

Boom.

Now, is it wrong to play video games? Of course not. Carter is saying that, in order to be exceptional, we must do the things that others aren't willing to do. And to his point, many people are not willing to grab a book instead of a controller.

If reading doesn't come naturally to you, don't worry. It's a skill, a habit, and a hobby that you can grow to love the more you do it. There are free library apps that allow access to eBooks, and there are tons of free audiobooks too.

Once you find a book you like, do an online search for books that are similar, or perhaps read more books by the same author.

Being a millionaire might not be your ultimate goal but applying success habits will help you reach whatever dream is on your heart. Adopt self-care habits to strengthen yourself physically, mentally, and emotionally, and eventually you'll see a correlation with how you succeed financially.

laser focused

I have no doubt that you are probably well aware of how difficult it can be to stay focused. The ability to stay on task without being sidetracked is definitely easier for some than others. However, we must recognize that staying focused is a challenge, but it is only the first part of the process. The next part is even harder. *Practicing being focused.* For those without a medical issue, the practice of staying on one task at a time and remaining focused will help to develop a good habit, one that can be carried through adulthood.

When we are focused on one goal, we stay on a straight path. This straight path keeps us grounded and on track. You need this, son. It's so important to keep your eye on the prize without allowing yourself to get distracted by friends, girls, or anything else that may present itself.

> **"The greater the success, the more it was due to one thing: focus."**[17]
> SHANE PARRISH

Staying focused also involves stopping regularly to reevaluate and reflect on your goals. Write them down and review them often. You can't meet a goal if you don't know what it is. Once the goal is specific and concrete, then you can put a deadline on it. A goal without a deadline is just a dream. Whether the goal is physical, such as being able to bench press 255 pounds—or academic, like scoring a 32 on your ACT—once it's established, you can set a deadline that will keep you working hard and moving forward.

Setting the goal and deadline will help you accomplish more than if you failed to set it in the first place. Even if you don't reach the goal, you'll be much closer to meeting it than if you didn't try at all. I've heard it said that those who shoot for the moon will land among the stars. I think that's a pretty good phrase to hold on to!

effective leadership
is putting
first things first.
effective management
is discipline,
carrying it out.

STEPHEN COVEY

16

the secrets of
time management

Want to know the secret of being on time?

Prepare. Prepare. Prepare.

Hate early mornings? Set your clothes out, including socks and shoes. Make sure your keys are in the proper spot. Be aware of the location of your wallet. And print out or grab any documents or items that you'll need to bring.

Congrats—you've just cut your morning rush in half! All you have to do now is wake up, perform your bathroom duties, get dressed, and grab some grub before heading out the door.

By investing a few minutes into preparation, you've now saved yourself stress and anxiety, and you've allowed for the possibility that your alarm doesn't go off on time. (Or, even worse, you don't hear it.)

> "Success depends upon previous preparation, and without such preparation there is sure to be failure."[18]
>
> CONFUCIUS

Another thought on prepping: Be sure you have everything handy before you head out the door. It's too easy to *think* you have everything you need, only to arrive at school, work, or soccer practice and realize your shin guards are on the floor of your bedroom.

To prevent this at the Jett house, we've set a rule. At the risk of all the jokes that could arise, here it is: *Touch it.*

Touch your lunch. Touch your homework. Touch your PE clothes. If you can't touch it, you don't have it.

Another way to ensure you arrive somewhere on time is to leave early, which is *always* easier said than done.

In the military, it's a common joke that every commanding officer tells their team to arrive fifteen minutes earlier than what is scheduled. So if the top-ranking officer says to show up at 0700 hours (or 7 a.m.), each leader passes down an extra fifteen-minute window through the ranks to make sure their people are on time. 0700 becomes 0645, which turns into 0630, and so on. By the time it gets to the lowest ranking member, the arrival time is 0500 hours (5 a.m.)

and that servicemember stands alone in the wee hours of the morning, wondering why no one else has arrived.

The fifteen-minute rule will save you countless headaches and embarrassment, and it allows for any unforeseen situations. Traffic will build up. The car will break down. So give yourself a buffer. You'll never regret it.

the swinging pendulum

ossibly one of the most difficult things to do today is to find balance. If you listen to adults talk long enough, you'll hear us talk about how hard it is to have balance. Many times, we struggle to find balance because we work too much and then we don't have any time reserved for our families. Or we commit so much time to a hobby that we neglect our friendships. We can often swing in either direction like a pendulum and easily spend the rest of our lives running in multiple directions, looking to restore balance.

As a young person who hopes to develop good habits and understand the challenges of adulthood, it's important to keep an eye on balance in your own life. Try to develop a constant practice of assessing your use of time, money, and resources.

It's also important to understand that sometimes things will go out of balance on purpose. However, this should only be for short periods of time and not develop into a lifestyle. For example, sometimes we work extra hours to pay off a big bill or save money for a big purchase. This might require working so much that we don't see our families or friends for a while. Sometimes we invest a lot of time into physical exercise because we are trying to earn a scholarship for school, and this might cause us to be thrown out of balance since we are trying to level up our abilities. Other times we have to budget our money so we can pay for essentials, such as food, shelter, and our vehicle, and that means we may not go eat out with friends or spend money on activities and fun.

We can achieve balance through having the right motivations. These motivations can be both external and internal. External motivations might come from our family or teachers, but internal motivations—the ones that come from the deep places within us—those are the ones that matter most!

> "Pursuing your goal is, in a sense, fired by internal motivation. Hence, you need a source of external motivation to keep things in balance."[19]
>
> BEN ROBINSON

Keeping an eye on the goal and striving to remain balanced will be a lifelong pursuit. Since it's a journey, I advise starting now. That way, you can recognize the possible issues you might have, and then you can work to bring your life and decisions into balance as much as you can.

have the heart of a teacher

L ife is a giant circle of not knowing anything, thinking you know everything, and then eventually realizing that you don't really know anything at all.

In fact, it's a sign of intelligence to realize how much you *don't* know, and it's a sign of maturity to admit it.

> "A thinker sees his own actions as experiments and questions—as attempts to find out something. Success and failure are for him answers above all."[20]
>
> FRIEDRICH NIETZSCHE

We learn many lessons from our mistakes, as well as the mistakes of others. Failure isn't something to fear; rather, it is a potential rite of passage we face when venturing into new waters.

Rarely, if ever, was an invention created on first attempt. In fact, many wonderful things we love today were the result of an accident. Chocolate chip cookies, sticky notes, penicillin … the list goes on.

And the final piece of this puzzle is actually a balancing act: Don't ever dumb yourself down in order to make someone else feel better and don't inflate your sense of self-importance in order to make others feel less-than.

The heart of a teacher is to help others understand, and in many ways, we are all teachers, although not all by profession. We learn from those who know more; in turn, we then pass that knowledge down to others.

If we're hoping to receive praise, adoration, or the mere glory of being the smartest person in the room, we're not leaning into the heart of a teacher.

The bottom line? Don't apologize for being smart, or for mastering a skill, and be sure to pass your knowledge on so you can help others achieve their own success.

never stop learning

> "Develop a passion for learning.
> If you do, you will never cease to grow."[21]
>
> ANTHONY J. D'ANGELO

At what age does it become no longer cool to admit you like going to school? Don't ask me; I'm not sure, considering I've always enjoyed learning, and school was a great place to do that! No, I didn't like the quizzes and tests or even the research projects, but there was great joy that came with learning new things. I loved learning new material that made me think differently or use my imagination in a new way.

Unfortunately, there seems to be a time when admitting you enjoy learning becomes something you no longer want to share with your friends. You no longer raise your hand to answer questions, and you act like you don't want to learn new things. Maybe you tell your friends you only like going to school because it's an excuse to get out of the house and see your friends.

I wish that weren't the case, because the truth is, our entire lives consist of learning! This process of learning continues because there never comes a time when we stop learning and growing.

Instead, we should absolutely embrace learning and enjoy it! Yes, I understand that studying for exams, writing research papers, and creating science projects may not be the most fun; however, the actual learning process itself can be exciting. The process of reading for the pure joy of it, or researching (*googling* is more like it), in an effort to learn more about how something is performed or created, expands our minds and our horizons. Don't let what others think about your desire to learn steal your natural joy to learn, and apply, new things.

you don't succeed
by being perfect.
you succeed
by doing
good work
consistently.

THIBAUT

perception, obedience, and communication

> "What you see and what you hear depends a great deal on where you are standing."[22]
>
> C.S. LEWIS, in *The Magician's Nephew*

Perception is reality.

This lesson has stuck with me since my days working at a major Orlando hospital. The orientation trainer explained to us that, you may have worked a twelve-hour shift without breaks—but the second a patient sees you standing around and *not* helping them, their perception is that you're being lazy or don't care about your job. It's not what is *actually* happening that's important; rather, it's what the person will believe.

This is where the concept of grace comes into play, and this will serve you well in most areas of life. Be quick to give people the benefit of the doubt and slow to assume the worst.

In order to implement this same philosophy in your own behavior, remember this adage: *Slow obedience is disobedience.*

For instance, if your parent tells you to clean your room and instead you spend the next five minutes finishing a video game match or texting a friend, then the perception from the parent's point of view is that you're being disobedient and disrespectful ... and that can quickly lead to a punishment.

The reality of the situation was that you just needed a couple of minutes to finish what you were doing. From your perspective, it's unfair to receive punishment.

This is where clear communication comes in handy.

With regard to the "video game, clean your room" situation, think about how much better the interaction could play out if it instead went like this:

Mom: "Go clean your room."

You: "I've got six minutes left in this match. Can I finish first? And then I'll go straight there."

Regardless of how your mom responds, you're demonstrating maturity by asking for permission. You've acknowledged her request (or command, however you see it), and you've explained and asked for more time using specific language.

Then, if your mom grants the extra time, you can build trust by following through. But when the game is over, you better get your butt up and go clean the room (or whatever chore you've been given).

This builds a habit that will spill into the workplace as you grow.

Your boss will assign tasks, and if he or she doesn't think you're moving on with those responsibilities, they may reprimand you. Or they could refrain from saying anything, but when time comes for promotions and raises, you're the one who gets passed over.

So, what's the lesson here?

Be careful about how you present yourself and use clear, specific communication; that way, you remain in the good graces of those who control your fate. (That's a pretty great place to be, if you ask me!)

lock the doors

One of the best gifts you could give yourself and your future family is the gift of safety. I still remember the sounds of my dad's nightly routine as he checked every lock on each door in my childhood home before he would head to his room for the night.

For my dad, the reassurance that the house was locked brought so much security. I didn't realize how safe I'd felt as a child until I left home and became responsible for my own door-locking routine.

However, there is more to safety than simply locking the doors at night. This type of safety involves remaining aware of your surroundings and avoiding places and situations where you could become a victim.

> A popular safety saying from the early 1900s said, "Do not think because an accident hasn't happened to you that it can't happen."

There's no secret that we're distracted these days more than ever. Instead of paying attention to our surroundings, our eyes are instead focused on our phones, and our ears are tuned in to music, podcasts, or a voice on the other end of a phone call. Is there anyone who pays attention to their surroundings?

Bad guys do.

Make no mistake: The easiest victims are the ones who can be taken by surprise or won't fight back.

This is just one of many reasons we shouldn't consume an inappropriate amount of alcohol (legally, of course) or do drugs. Don't let anything impair your judgment and refuse to place yourself in a situation where you wouldn't be able to adequately protect yourself.

Along the same lines, try to demonstrate your maturity by being a safe driver—yes, even in your teen years. Speeding doesn't make anyone comfortable. Too many deaths and accidents have occurred in exchange for a few minutes of being "cool" or trying to shave a few minutes off the drive time. The end result *is not* worth it.

One day, if you choose to have a family, it will be more than just your life on the line. You'll want to provide the protection and comfort that comes from being safety-minded, and that habit can start now.

it's ok to lose but we play to win

articipation trophies are great for those little kids who are learning to play a sport. They learned teamwork, athletic skills, and, really, who is concerned with the win-loss record of four-year-olds?

At some point, though, the gloves come off, as it were, and a win-loss means something.

> "In an attempt to promote equality we have robbed our youth of the most growth-inducing aspect of competition, failing. Losing, in the

context of whatever arena it may be, is a microcosmic death. When we learn from our failures and grow because of them, we are reborn."[23]

CHRIS MATAKAS, Brazilian Jiu Jitsu specialist

While it might sound a little dramatic, Matakas is completely right. It's the mistakes, the mess-ups, and the failures that teach us the most valuable lessons in life.

Here at the Jett house, there are three rules we follow while playing games:

1. It's okay to lose, but play to win.
2. Shake hands and say *congratulations*.
3. No sore losers or braggy winners.

There's competition everywhere we go. We can choose to either be a healthy competitor or sulk and whine if we don't win or get our way. The way in which we handle disappointment is a major character trait that we can work on, and honestly, learning to embrace defeat and loss without the rage-quitting is a skill to be mastered. Can you imagine losing a client in a business meeting and responding by kicking over a chair and throwing a notebook across the room?

Talk about getting fired pretty quickly!

Use the opportunities that come your way to practice your response to both winning and losing, and then be gracious with whatever outcome you face.

CHAPTER **23**

nothing is free

othing is truly free. Everything comes at a cost.

That buy-one-get-one-free offer? Not truly free. Stores will discount certain products to where they're actually losing money just to get you to come in and buy more. This strategy is called using "loss leaders," and it can be quite effective.

What's free for you wasn't necessarily free for someone else.

> "There is no such thing as free lunch."[24]
>
> MILTON FRIEDMAN, Nobel Laureate

Even if you are given a literal zero-dollar cheeseburger platter, there is still something called *opportunity cost*. This means that each decision costs you an opportunity based on your choice. If you eat that zero-dollar burger meal, you will, in the process, give up the opportunity to eat something different.

While this doesn't sound like a difficult choice or sacrifice, when it comes to understanding finance and economics, the opportunity cost is an innate part of the equation.

In the same manner, even gifts can come at a cost—so be wise. Are there strings attached? Is there an expectation of return on your part? What do you have to give, either tangibly, like money—or intangibly, like time? Will it cost your integrity? Character? Your good name?

As you make decisions on how to handle your time and finances, keep the costs in mind. Consider the other opportunities you'll be saying *no* to—even if those opportunities are merely monetary and emotional.

Choose to work hard; that way, you're eventually able to provide for yourself, your future family, and you can be someone who can give without strings attached. Then some day you can be the person who provides someone a chance at a zero-dollar lunch.

leaders aren't born,
they are made.
and they are made just
like anything else,
through hard work.
and that's the
price we'll have to pay
to achieve that goal,
or any goal.

VINCE LOMBARDI

the credit trap

hen you see a representative on campus touting a complimentary T-shirt—or something worthless, like a squishy stress ball—do an about-face and walk the other direction. Don't sign up for a free bank account, credit card, phone plan, or anything else that requires you to share your personal information with a complete stranger in the name of freebies.

> **"Never spend your money before you earned it."**[25]
>
> **THOMAS JEFFERSON**

This sounds simple when you hear it, but it's so hard to do in reality. Don't you agree? The appeal to hold on to our cash and still gain access to something we want is extremely strong.

Companies know this, which is why there are ample opportunities to *buy now, pay later.* One of the biggest mistakes and deepest holes you can get yourself into is credit card debt. At some point you will need to build credit; but too often, instead of building your credit to a healthy score, it becomes tanked by maxing out cards or missing a payment.

Another way people often become trapped is through interest. This refers to a percentage of money you pay on top of the original purchase. The interest can quickly accumulate into a sum that you would never spend on the actual product. As an example, let's say you're starving and the college cafeteria is closed, and eating another bowl of ramen just can't cut it.

Boom. Pizza.

Well, that late-night pizza cost you $14 on your "emergencies-only" credit card. After all, your parents don't want you to starve, right? But if you don't pay off your credit card balance, the interest will start to accrue. Depending on how much you charge to that card, and how long it takes for you to pay it off, there's a chance that the $14 pizza could end up costing $30 or more over time.

One trick for building self-discipline in finances is to save double the price of the item you want before you buy it. Here's how this would work: If you want the newest video game console that costs $499, then you'd need to save $999 before buying it.

Sounds terrible, right? After all, it's hard enough to save the $499. So let's cut the amount to save a little. If the console is $499, let's say you'd have to save at least 25% of the amount. That would be an extra $124.75. And don't forget, we haven't factored in the taxes or potential shipping for the item either.

Here's the gist.

Work hard for your money. Save more than you spend. Sell what you don't need. And try to pay cash (or use your debit card) whenever possible.

what's in a name?

hether it's a name like Elon Musk or Theodore Roosevelt, O.J. Simpson or Bill Gates, people often associate a name with a particular act or acts. Each of these people are known throughout history or in our society for what they did *or didn't do*.

It's difficult to regain a good reputation after it's been tarnished. It's difficult to prove yourself after you have become known as a liar, cheater, or thief.

It's much easier to protect your good name and reputation by living above and resisting the temptation to do wrong things.

Although you likely won't grow up to become murderers, you can still become known as someone who is untrustworthy, unreliable, and a fake friend. None of us want to be known for being that type of a person, but we don't always take the necessary steps to intentionally develop the *opposite* traits.

What do I mean by that?

Don't be an untrustworthy person—instead, tell the truth!

Don't be unreliable—instead, be the kind of person who others can consistently count on. Make your word count—even if it hurts.

Don't be a fake friend—instead, be loyal, even when it requires sacrifices. In the end, I promise it will make a difference!

And if you've been judged unfairly by your friends or family members, your school, or anyone else, remember that it is your *character* that matters above all else. Our reputations can be beaten up and broken down at the whims of people who don't have good morals, but our character is ours alone to protect. It matters the most!

> "Be more concerned with your character than with your reputation, because your character is what you really are, while your reputation is merely what others think you are."[26]
>
> JOHN WOODEN

CHAPTER **26**

keep your word

A gentleman's agreement, or *handshake agreement*, is a situation in which an understanding is reached without the need for a legal document. In other words, each party trusts the other to keep their part of the contract.

First and foremost, in all cases regarding business and finance, don't rely on a gentleman's agreement. Get every agreement down in writing. Why? Because anyone who works within the law will tell you, "If it wasn't written down, it doesn't exist."

That said, when it comes to being a man of integrity, your word is your reputation, and once it's tarnished, it can be difficult to regain the original luster.

This really comes into play with non-legal issues. Integrity reveals itself most in situations that could allow you to "get away" with something wrong, but instead you choose to do the right thing.

> "In looking for people to hire, look for three qualities: integrity, intelligence, and energy. And if they don't have the first, the other two will kill you."[27]
>
> WARREN BUFFET

In the Chinese folktale "The Emperor's Seed,"[28] the emperor has a competition to find his next heir. He gives every child a seed, and then he tells the children to return in a year so he can judge their plants. A boy named Ling watered and cared for his plant every day, but it never sprouted.

On the day of the choosing, every kid had a plant in his pot—every kid, however, except for Ling. Turns out, the seeds that the Emperor had given to the kids were nonviable. They were *never* going to grow. Since Ling was the only one who didn't have a plant, the Emperor knew Ling had a strong sense of integrity and chose him to be the heir.

While the majority of deals and agreements in your life won't be tricks or competitions to find out how much integrity you have, there are still hundreds of decisions you make every day, choices that can someday come back to either haunt or help your reputation.

Choose the right path, even if the outcome doesn't seem like it will come out in your favor. In the long run, it will get you farther in life than cheating. I'll shake on it.

true humility

> "Humility is not thinking less of yourself,
> it's thinking of yourself less."[29]
>
> RICK WARREN

You walk a fine line as a young man. I know it can't be easy for you to try to navigate your future, juggle responsibilities, or learn everything you need to know in this life. And although exhibiting confidence is a necessary commodity, lacking humility should never be desirable!

Being humble isn't the same thing as being insecure and lacking confidence. Rather, being humble requires that we become more focused on others' happiness and comfort.

When we're humble, this means that the center of our attention is not on ourselves; rather, it's zoned in on those around us—their cares, needs, and concerns. How can we develop an others-focused mindset? We can begin by getting involved in community service, actively helping someone in need, being a listening ear when a friend has a problem, or even doing a sibling's chore on their behalf.

> **"Humility is throwing oneself away in complete concentration on something or someone else."[30]**
> MADELEINE L'ENGLE

When you keep others first and treat them better than you treat yourself, then you can't go wrong.

And when you treat others well, that's when you can walk with confidence, knowing that you are a man marked by humility—a man who will be honored by others as he becomes known for his generosity.

CHAPTER **28**

ask for help
... and directions

b e secure enough in your manhood to use the GPS, ask for help when needed, and read the assembly directions. Why waste time building something, only to approach the end and then realize that several "extra" parts weren't utilized?

In the same manner, why drive around in circles when you can simply open a maps app on your phone, follow directions, and arrive at your destination?

There is nothing cool about getting lost or wasting time. In fact, the opposite is true. People who refuse to ask for help become so ingrained in their so-called independent ideal that, eventually, the people who love them most stop offering them assistance.

Avoid this trap. Know your limits. Asking for help doesn't make you look weak. It makes you look *secure.*

> **"Asking for help does not mean that we are weak or incompetent. It usually indicates an advanced level of honesty and intelligence."**[31]
>
> DR. ANNE WILSON SCHAEF

That's a mic drop moment.

There is a stigma, particularly for men, that asking for help is a sign they can't handle the situation or aren't smart enough to figure it out. A leader doesn't concern himself with the presumed optics; instead, he focuses on the task at hand and educates himself.

Open the manual.

Watch a tutorial.

Call a friend.

Or even better—call a parent. After all, these are the people who love you, raised you, and guided you, and I bet they love nothing more than to impart their wisdom to their children. Lean on the experience of others. Learn from their mistakes.

be Fearless

Be Bold! Be Fearless! Be Courageous!

Easier said than done, right? Sometimes, being bold—going against the crowd, your peers, or the norm of society—can be downright frightening.

But many times the thing we fear will happen never does. We think, if we don't go to that party, then all of our friends will abandon us. Sure, some might, but not everyone. (And if they do, perhaps they weren't meant to be in our lives to begin with.) In fact, by taking a stand, you may even meet new people who actually want to become your friend because of your boldness. Being fearless means that you are willing to take that risk. If people abandon you or talk behind your back, then at least you know you were man enough to take that stand.

And truth be told, that's actual manhood, isn't it? I'm not referring to being fearless in the face of danger, or while doing stupid things, but rather being bold enough to take a stand—especially when it may not be popular to do so. *That* is true manliness.

A real man is the same in private as he is in public. He says what he means and means what he says. He stands for truth, for kindness, and for justice. Be that kind of young man. Be *fearless*!

Can I let you in on a little secret? Being fearless involves taking action in spite of feeling afraid. It doesn't actually mean that you don't experience the actual emotion of fear. Sometimes we just move forward, anyway, even though doing so might scare us to death.

> "If we take the generally accepted definition of bravery as a quality which knows no fear, I have never seen a brave man. All men are frightened. The more intelligent they are, the more they are frightened."[32]
>
> GEORGE S. PATTON

CHAPTER **30**

think FOR yourself

We are living in the day and age of what is referred to as *groupthink*. The ability we have to remain anonymous behind a screen grants us the freedom to wait and keep an eye on a controversial social media conversation. That way, we can see how the majority of people respond on the topic before we comment with our own opinion.

It's becoming increasingly harder for us to share an unpopular opinion. Trolls have no mercy, and it seems as though they're always on the hunt for their next victim.

This mob mentality, where people act in ways totally against their nature when they're part of a bigger group, means we can feel threatened, attacked, and crucified by strangers simply for sharing a different viewpoint.

It takes strength to say what you believe, regardless of how unpopular that belief may be. In fact, the danger really lies in staying silent. Withholding your voice puts you on a slippery slope that can lead to giving up your rights.

> "Think for yourself, or others will think for you without thinking of you."[33]
>
> HENRY DAVID THOREAU

He's totally right. Never forget that you are the best advocate for you.

Along these lines, not only do you need to have the guts to say what you believe, but you also need to know *why* you believe it. Can you back up your views? Can you have a conversation with someone who doesn't share your thoughts?

Know this: You may not be popular when you share what you think, but all too often, things come back around. And trust me—you will want to be on the right side of history when they do.

a man who wants to **lead the ORCHESTRA** must turn his back on **the crowd.**

MAX LUCADO

CHAPTER **31**

practice
diligence

Practicing diligence requires not only staying on task in the moment, but also preparing our bodies physically and mentally in advance. These wise choices condition us to remain sharp in the big decisions we need to make, the answers we need to remember, and the work that needs to be done.

But let's face it—it's not always easy to be diligent in today's world. And truth be told, it's *never* been easy to be diligent, but it seems far more challenging today than ever before. Distractions bombard us from all corners—streaming shows, social media, and video games, just to name a few. There are sports and after-school activities, and while those may be good within themselves, they can still cause us to show slack in other priorities—such as schoolwork, chores, and jobs.

Sometimes we scroll through Tik Tok videos too long, or play video games for hours on end, without even realizing how much time has slipped by.

Sometimes we invest so much of ourselves into sports and hanging out with our friends, and then we have no energy left to complete our school assignments, study for tests, or do our work without dragging our feet.

Procrastination on our important tasks almost always hurts us in the end; being diligent forces us to avoid this harmful trait.

> "The leading rule for the lawyer, as for the man of every other calling, is diligence. Leave nothing for to-morrow which can be done to-day."[34]
>
> ABRAHAM LINCOLN

We often sacrifice sleep when we neglect to put the phones away, the controllers down, and turn off the screens. Lack of sleep not only affects our physical bodies but our diligence as well. It keeps us from having a clear mind to perform the tasks we should be focused on. A lack of rest can be damaging in so many ways!

Be a young man who will remain diligent in his responsibilities. You will not regret it!

CHAPTER **32**

do it right or do it twice

Mr. Jett's favorite saying is, "Do it right or do it twice," which is basically his version of my "touch it once" rule. This means that, if you pick something up, you can't set it down in the wrong spot because then you'll have to go back and pick it up again. Touch it *once* and take care of it at that time.

Both phrases are ones we can live by because they can save *soooooooooo* much time in the long run. And time, my friend, is precious, and it doesn't provide refunds.

Another one of his favorite sayings accompanies the first: "Slow is steady, and steady is fast."

Taking our time is a difficult skill to master because it fights against our hurry-up-and-wait mentality.

> "The two most powerful warriors
> are patience and time."[35]
>
> LEO TOLSTOY, author of *War and Peace*

Used together, patience and time are incredible weapons we can keep in our toolbelt.

The ability to demonstrate self-control, particularly under pressure, is a skill you can learn and improve upon. Take military snipers as an example. Part of their training requires that they move slowly and methodically as they learn to "stalk." It's said that sniper teams sometimes lie in the same position for days if needed. That type of dedication, patience, and ability to demonstrate self-control is a learned behavior. This means we, too, can practice these skills on a daily basis.

Finally, along with the "Do it right or do it twice" motto is another goodie: "Practice until you can't get it wrong." This may sound a little off since many people would advise, "Practice until you get it right." But during my time as an assistant cheer coach, we wanted our athletes to practice until the moves became ingrained in their heads and muscle memory; that way, there is little chance for them to do the form or performance incorrectly.

Slow is steady. Steady is fast. And your time is worth

devoting the extra effort required so that you will not have to redo your work.

on honesty

onesty is a rare trait to have today. It used to be the norm that people were generally honest in their dealings with each other. Unfortunately, that is no longer the case. Perhaps even the reverse is true, as we have become more skeptical of others in our society.

In today's culture, it's unusual to avoid telling a "little white lie" to cover your tracks when trying to avoid coming clean with the truth.

Can I encourage you for a moment?

Don't lose a passion for honesty.

Your honesty can mark you as a special, even remarkable, individual, someone who is to be trusted and relied upon. Resist the pressure that will be placed on you to go along with the crowd and to be anything less than honest. Don't fall for the thinking that no one will ever know.

Truth is always revealed in the end.

You can't plant weeds and expect a beautiful harvest of tomatoes, cucumbers, and squash. Instead, you always reap what you sow, and dishonesty is a terrible weed. If you plant a field of tomatoes, you won't reap corn. The same is true in our dealings with others. The minute you begin to be less than honest, it's incredibly difficult to convince people of your honesty in the future.

> "Each time you are honest and conduct yourself with honesty, a success force will drive you toward greater success. Each time you lie, even with a little white lie, there are strong forces pushing you toward failure." [36]
>
> JOSEPH SUGARMAN

Your character is so very important. Hold yourself to a higher standard and be honest, even when it hurts.

don't light your pants on Fire ... even a little

Trust is like a vase. Strong, sturdy, beautiful, and extremely fragile.

Do you remember the fable, "The Boy Who Cried 'Wolf'?" In the story, a boy would take the sheep out every day and yell, "Wolf! Wolf!" and the townspeople ran to help. But he wasn't being truthful; a wolf was nowhere in sight. The boy laughed and laughed at his ability to fool everyone. He repeated this joke for several days, and eventually the townspeople grew weary of these lies.

Then one day, a wolf actually did show up—and when the boy yelled for help, the townspeople never came. Why?

Well, they assumed he was telling yet another lie. And you can just imagine what happened next.

> "When we tell little white lies, we become progressively color-blind. It is better to remain silent than to mislead."[37]
>
> JAMES E. FAUST

A white lie is still a half-truth. It's a gray area, which can sometimes be a little confusing. If you lie to a friend because you're trying to surprise them, did you *actually* lie? What if you're a super-secret spy with top security clearance? What if you're an undercover cop?

How legalistic do we need to be when it comes to what a lie is and what it isn't?

Surprise parties and spies aside, a good rule of thumb is to consider the motivation behind the falsehood.

If your intent is to deceive, then you might want to reconsider. In fact, telling the truth in small situations helps you to build trust, and this trust can come in handy when you find yourself in a major situation and need people to believe you. By choosing not to lie over the "small things," you will show yourself to be someone who is trustworthy, and that trust holds more and more weight over time.

That said, if you've damaged a relationship because of lies, it's time to make amends. Repairing trust takes time because you've broken the "vase of trust," but over time you can put the pieces back together.

CHAPTER 35

Revolutionary truth

It's always easier to lie than to tell the truth. It's our natural inclination to try to protect ourselves too. Lie to cover our weakness, lie to mask our failures, lie to hide our tracks when we get caught.

But if you want to lead an exceptional life, one that is countercultural, then you will strive to live in an honest manner.

> "In a time of deceit telling the truth is a revolutionary act."[38]
>
> GEORGE ORWELL

Speaking truth, even when it hurts, is an important habit to develop. But it's a habit that you *must* develop in order to counter our instinct to lie.

Even more so, we're presented with a challenge in today's society to tell the truth *with an added measure of kindness and love*. You might very well be right in your words, but when you sling them around recklessly, you can risk hurting people. It is essential that you balance your truthful words with both kindness and gentleness.

You will have to tell the truth, yet you will need to temper your tone with kindness.

You will have to face consequences for your actions or lack of action.

You will sometimes face the decision to tell the truth or tell a lie, knowing that no one would ever know the difference if you weren't honest.

But if you want to avoid this massive pothole on your way to adulthood, you'll start to develop this muscle now. The more you practice being honest, truthful, *and kind,* the easier it will become, and the more you will become known for your choice of words.

You will begin to develop friends you can count on, people who will rely on you and trust you because of your truthfulness. Start now to build this circle of friends by creating a pattern of being a truthful man.

you gain
**strength, courage
and confidence**
by every experience in
which you really stop to
look fear in the face.
you must
do the thing
you think
you cannot do.

ELEANOR ROOSEVELT

where'd i put my moral compass?

ntegrity differs from honesty because of the added layer of morality. Living to a standard that could otherwise be called a "moral compass." While others around you live in a way that makes them feel good or happy, young men who hope to make a difference will hold themselves to a higher standard. A moral compass can help you to stay on track when others distract or try to bring you down to their level. Just like how a GPS guides us to our preferred destination, a moral compass helps to guide us in life's decisions.

By avoiding lying and embracing honesty, you will take a step toward living with morality. Integrity takes this even farther down the path because it involves that you speak up when you see that something is wrong.

Integrity is standing up for what you know is right, no matter the cost.

Integrity involves making a difference in the world, no matter your age.

It's not just about being honest and trustworthy; rather, it's the highest moral character that may require you to stand up for those who are bullied, mistreated, and rejected.

And this is what true leadership looks like. A true leader is known for his integrity, his presence under fire, and his compassion for others. A true leader doesn't wait to be invited to lead; instead, he takes charge because he understands the need and is willing to help. A leader doesn't count his own cost; rather, he understands that sometimes sacrifices are required when serving others.

A person who has no integrity, or no moral compass, can easily be dragged down by people who only want to destroy him. In the guise of friendship, these individuals do nothing to elevate or inspire, but instead they seek to bring that person down to their level. Drugs, violence, and addictions of all kinds can stem from a complete lack of moral character. When we have good morality, we have a standard of right and wrong. And by determining to hold yourself to that standard, you will become a young man who is worthy of leading.

the
supreme quality
of leadership is
integrity.

DWIGHT EISENHOWER

CHAPTER **39**

leadership
potential

> "Leadership is not magnetic personality, that can just as well be a glib tongue. It is not 'making friends and influencing people,' that is flattery. Leadership is lifting a person's vision to higher sights, the raising of a person's performance to a higher standard, the building of a personality beyond its normal limitations."[40]
>
> PETER F. DRUCKER

aybe you are the class president or a team captain.

Or maybe you wish you were.

In either case, I can tell you that being a leader is a lot of work. While it may seem like leaders have it easier, the truth is that leaders—especially the good ones—are entrusted with more responsibility and often must work harder than others.

I've heard professional athletes asked, in interviews, about their thoughts on being a role model for young children. They respond with something along the lines of, "I never asked to be that." But the reality is that young children will look up to people who are considered as leaders. They will frame their lifestyle and decisions after celebrities, athletes, and influencers whom they admire, those they witness achieving success—even if that person never asked for that type of responsibility.

Did you know you are considered a leader as well? Maybe it's to your younger sibling, cousin, niece or nephew, or peers from your school. There are always going to be younger kids who look up to you. They will witness how you behave, and like it or not, they may try to be just like you.

When I was younger, the "Be Like Mike" campaign was very popular. Michael Jordan's name was synonymous with *greatness*. As his platform grew beyond sports, he became known outside of strictly the basketball world. He became a phenomenon that everyone recognized, young and old alike.

Think about it:

Should adults advise younger people to model your

behavior, speech, and decisions? Would the "Be Like (insert your name here)" campaign be a winner or a dud?

Be worthy of being imitated. *That's* what defines true leadership.

Privilege, Responsibility, and Hard Work

> "The heights by great men reached and kept were not attained in sudden flight, but they while their companions slept, they were toiling upwards in the night."[41]
>
> HENRY WADSWORTH LONGFELLOW

It should come as no surprise to you that with privilege comes more responsibility. Working through the summers, doing a few extra odd jobs throughout the school year, and saving furiously can lead to that first car. Then once you have a car, you have to keep earning if you hope to keep it gassed up, covered by insurance, and clean! And don't forget that a car also needs a tag and maintenance, such as oil changes, tires, and more.

Like it or not, that's the constant balancing act you will face for the rest of your life. Whether you are working to take care of your own needs—or if you are caring for a family—you will bear responsibility for providing that food, shelter, and basic needs.

But shouldering responsibility is part of the privilege as well. It is a privilege to drive where and when you want, and that is balanced by the responsibility of caring for that car.

The key you want to remember is this: Privilege and responsibility go hand in hand with hard work. Without devoting hard work, it wouldn't be possible to enjoy the privilege. Yes, this means you may have to work while others are playing. You may have to prepare now so you can protect your future later. And you may have to go without and save more than you spend; that way, you can take care of your responsibilities in the future too. It's so worth it though!

Be the man that shoulders responsibility well!

take
responsibility

here are two situations in life when you should most definitely keep your mouth shut: at the scene of an accident, and if you're taken into custody or interrogated by the police.

Even uttering the words "I'm sorry" can land you in unwanted trouble, and in the case of a car accident, saying this could potentially result in a ticket.

While this may sound shocking and a little dishonest, let me be clear: If you make an apology at the scene of an accident—whether it be a fender bender or something more serious—then anyone who hears you can claim, in their witness statement for record, that you have taken responsibility for the damage. And when you file your car insurance claim, you may not end up with the coverage you need, the coverage you paid for, or the coverage you deserve.

"The victim mindset dilutes the human potential. By not accepting personal responsibility for our circumstances, we greatly reduce our power to change them."[42]

STEVE MARABOLI, military veteran, bestselling author, behavioral science academic, and "The Most Quoted Man Alive," according to *Inc.* magazine)

Many lawyers will tell you that the best thing you can do, in this type of situation, is to make sure everyone involved is okay. Call the police. Help where needed. And then give your statement to the authorities.

The same is true if you're ever, God forbid, arrested or questioned by the police. Take a look at the first part of the Miranda Rights warning, which authorities are required to tell anyone who is being arrested: "You have the right to remain *silent.* Anything you say *can* and *will* be used *against* you."

In this case, your words won't help you; they will literally be used against you.

So, then, how can we take responsibility for our actions—a positive character trait—without taking responsibility for our actions when it comes to the law? Isn't this a contradiction?

No, it isn't, because this is why lawyers were created.

Taking responsibility doesn't require that we spill our guts and tell everything we know. It means that we look at the big picture, make smart choices, and find people we trust to help us make those decisions. And when there are consequences, we accept the punishment and move on.

CHAPTER **40**

listening to your parents and other authority figures

he ability to respect authority is a skill and life lesson
that should be learned early in life. You don't have to
like everyone necessarily, but you do have to respect the
position of the person who is in charge over you.

How you behave in public is a direct reflection on
your parents.

However, it's not always easy to respect people you don't
like. Maybe you've faced this struggle at school or work.
Respect often needs to be earned—or, at least, we feel like
it does. But even if you don't like the person you work for,
you should still strive to make your boss look good.

> **"Nothing is more despicable than respect based on fear."**[43]
>
> ALBERT CAMUS, French novelist and essayist

Ways to respect authority figures include (but are not limited to) the following:

1. Say ma'am or sir.
2. Maintain eye contact (without glaring or staring!).
3. Keep your posture strong and upright.
4. Listen.
5. Communicate clearly.

A great attitude will get you far in life. Promotions and opportunities are almost always granted to the person who will be a nice reflection of the company, and if applicable, the person in charge.

The opposite is also true. A negative demeanor can keep you from receiving bonuses and rewards. There are many times, as a parent, when I want to do something fun or offer a special treat to my kids—but their bad attitudes can zap that desire in a heartbeat.

I remember when my dad and I would disagree. Instead of back talking or getting lippy, I just listened, and then we moved on. If I had argued with him, the focus of the disagreement would have transitioned to my attitude instead of the topic at hand.

You don't have to agree with everyone, but you *do* have to choose how to handle yourself in those moments. Many times my dad would say his piece, and then the dispute would end. I still didn't agree with him, but I showed respect.

Then, and this is a big *then*, I would re-evaluate and try a different approach in an effort for him to change his mind. Most of the time the only reason this worked was because he felt respected and was able to hear my side.

I challenge you to try this some time. It's not foolproof by any means, but if you show the authoritative figure the respect they deserve, they will often reciprocate the same amount of respect to you.

It's often been said that life is 10 percent what happens to you and 90 percent how you react to it. Choose to look for the silver lining. Choose to focus on the good rather than the bad.

The right attitude is the key that can unlock doors you never knew could be opened to you. Show that R-E-S-P-E-C-T and watch those doors fly open.

Choosing Respect, Even When You Don't Understand

You might have a friend who talks down to their parents. Or maybe this friend mistreats teachers at your school. *You* might even be that person, whether you realize it or not. Respect for those in authority can be difficult as a teenager. You are on your way to becoming your own man. You will have plenty of privileges and responsibilities soon enough, but you aren't quite there yet. And so often, this friction is at the core of the disrespect you may show to others. You may think you know more than that authority figure, or maybe you could handle problems differently. You want to be trusted and granted more freedom

than what you have, and your way of resisting is by show-
ing disrespect.

> "Attitude is a choice. Happiness is a choice.
> Optimism is a choice. Kindness is a choice.
> Giving is a choice. Respect is a choice.
> Whatever choice you make makes you.
> Choose wisely."[44]
>
> ROY T. BENNETT

The problem is, you just haven't lived long enough or
gained enough life experience to understand where your parents or guardians are coming from. And they want you to live
long enough to do just that. But you still have a little way to
go—it takes time and experience to learn the lessons we have
learned. It requires that you trust your parents don't "have it
in" for you; rather, they want you to thrive and accomplish
more than they ever have.

In other words, we want you to be better than we were,
so we try to protect you from making our mistakes.

While that's not always the best way to parent, sometimes
it's the only thing we know to do. Trust that we don't put lim-
itations on you to hold you back or because we think you are
a little kid. Instead, we know you will bear plenty of responsibility very soon, and we want to protect you as long as we can!

the importance of accountability

h ow well do you accept correction? It doesn't matter who gives the correction—whether it's someone in authority, such as a parent or teacher, or a friend who tries to hold you accountable. It's the way you handle correction that is important.

> "Everyone makes mistakes; it's how you respond to correction that shows the level of your character."[45]
>
> AUTHOR UNKNOWN

But I don't know anyone who likes to be corrected. It's hard to hear sometimes, and it's a reminder that we don't always do things well. I think sometimes we'd rather live in denial and pretend we have it all together, when the reality is—we don't.

However, it can be so valuable to have a friend who is willing to offer a word to us when we are getting off track.

This is the sign of a true friend!

Learning to accept what often feels like criticism, as well as sharing a word with a friend, is important in relationships. Being a safe place for someone to express himself or herself is vital, and when we need correction it is always better to receive it from a friend rather than a stranger. We know they care about us and can listen—hopefully with an open heart.

Sadly, we don't always respond to correction from authority well either. While you are younger, your parents have to exhibit authority and correction in your life. If they don't do this well and hold you responsible for your actions, then your future may not be easy. You will continually have trouble with authority as an adult, and you could be challenged as you learn to deal with correction that comes from breaking the rules or even violating the law.

So learn to love correction; after all, it makes you a better man!

i cannot give you the
FORMULA FOR SUCCESS,
but i can give you the
FORMULA FOR FAILURE,
which is: try to
please everybody.

HERBERT SWOPE

own your emotions

eal men cry. Yes. I said it.

As cliché as it seems, it's 100 percent true. Confident men aren't afraid to show their emotions, particularly in situations where being emotional is appropriate. We have a wide range of emotions simply because we are human.

> "Too many men I know experience shame because society places pressure on them to withhold emotion: emotion and sensitivity is weak. I have found the opposite is true: emotion and sensitivity are what make us strong."[46]
>
> NATALIE BRENNER

I couldn't agree more.

It takes strength to be vulnerable. A *super macho* attitude gets old after a while. In order to build intimacy with someone—whether it's a friend, relative, or future spouse—you need to be willing to show what's going on inside your heart.

It doesn't make you weak.

As an example, can you imagine telling former professional wrestler, Dwayne "the Rock" Johnson—who was also the voice of Maui in the Disney movie *Moana*—that performing in the emotional or non-hypermasculine roles makes him wimpy?

Everyone has a range of emotions. Justin and I call it "the pendulum," because it's like the swinging part of a grandfather clock. As far as the pendulum swings in one direction, it will swing back the same amount.

If someone is super sweet, the pendulum swings high up on the sweetness scale—but the opposite is also true. The outrage can also be extremely high, even if it takes a long time for that pendulum to swing back.

Back-and-forth. Back-and-forth.

People who are pretty steady with their feelings might have a short swing in both their positive and negative energy.

Either way, to pretend like a "real man" doesn't have emotions is to deny the truth of your inner self. Our feelings still get hurt, no matter how old we become. While we don't cry as easily as we did when we were toddlers, our emotions don't leave us once we hit puberty.

I've seen Justin Jett cry three times. Once at the death of a friend, and twice when he passionately shared with me about the injustices he had witnessed.

Because his emotional pendulum doesn't often hit that tears-breaking-point, it made those moments even more powerful. It showed me how much those situations meant to him.

Choose carefully who you want to be vulnerable with, but be sure to allow yourself to be unguarded at times. The right people will protect your emotions and provide a safe space for you to share, and in turn, you can be a safe space for someone else.

Read the Room

ctive listening is a skill you would be wise to develop, and the earlier, the better. People communicate with more than mere words.

> "The most important thing in communication is hearing what isn't said."[47]
>
> PETER F. DRUCKER (a brilliant man who contributed largely to the foundations of modern management)

Being tone-deaf in society means you're not paying attention to what is going on in the world around you. Celebrities get accused of this when they showcase their high-class vacations during a pandemic when people are out of work. Politicians are tone-deaf when they attempt solidarity with their constituency by posting about their $14-a-pint-ice cream when many families are out of work and can't provide food on the table.

We've all seen this happen in real life. Think back to a time when maybe you were with a group of people, and someone said something inappropriate, and immediately everyone felt awkward.

You probably already understand this concept. If your parents are sitting at the dinner table and are surrounded by paperwork, appearing stressed, then it probably isn't the best time to ask for a raise on your allowance. If there is a pile of laundry on the couch and dishes overflowing in the sink, you may want to pitch in before asking for a ride to a friend's house or requesting extra time to play your video games.

You understand this instinctively because you know how to read your parents. That same intuition needs to be applied to other life situations as well. For instance, if your boss was just chewed out by *their* boss, that definitely wouldn't be a time to ask for a raise. You get the point.

However, this is not as easily done via social media. You can't read the room of your friends and followers because you're not with them in person. This is why it's important to stay up-to-date with what is going on in the world. What topics are trending? What issues are people dealing with?

And the big question that more people should ask themselves before they post something online is, "What is the objection or pushback that I might receive from this?"

Avoid the unnecessary pitfall of creating the awkward or inappropriate moment by reading the room and actively listening. You can do this by observing the world (the macro level), and by observing your corner of the world (the micro level).

Knowledge is power, and as we all know from Spiderman, knowledge comes with great responsibility. (Thank you, Uncle Ben.) If you can identify potential criticism first, then you can decide if it would be worth it to say, post, or do whatever is on your mind. The risk is worth the reward, shall we say.

make or break

ake a minute to stop thinking about your to-do list for today and give me your full attention, as this is extremely important to note:

Your friends will make or break you.

That sounds heavy, and I know you may think I'm exaggerating—but it's the truth. Your friends will either encourage you to do good things, strive hard for good grades, work at a job, be kind and humble, or they will drive you in the complete opposite direction.

If your friends encourage you to lie to your parents, break curfew, stop working hard to make good grades, or be unkind and disrespectful, then it's likely they are not good friends. If you have a friend who is known for being those things, even if you aren't, they will eventually rub off on you. And even if you are the strongest young person in the world, and their behavior doesn't affect you, others' perception of you can still be based on your friend's behavior. And while that's not fair, it's still the reality of life.

> **"No person is your friend who demands your silence, or denies your right to grow."**[48]
>
> ALICE WALKER

There's an old phrase that goes like this: "If you lie down with dogs, you'll get up with fleas." You might not have ever heard that one, but it is one that is so true and provides an accurate visual. If you hang out with the wrong friends, they will eventually rub off on you one way or another. Be careful who you bond with. It's far preferable to have just one friend who is faithful, loyal, and can help you become a better person, than a whole group of people whose entire purpose might just be to bring you down.

becoming the friend a good friend will choose

ou will become like the people you hang around, so ask yourself: Are you the kind of person who an amazing person is looking for?

Do you have the characteristics and temperament of someone who makes *and keeps* friends?

If we want to hang out with people who are kind, honest, and loyal, then we too must be kind, honest, and loyal.

It's as simple as that.

There will be people who come into your life that you will just click with. There's no explanation, rhyme, or reason for it. You just fit together, and it's easy. Friends like that are wonderful. Never take those friendships for granted.

But some people are choosier. They observe first, and then they act. These people are paying attention to how you treat others before they decide to cross your path.

> "Goodness is about character—integrity, honesty, kindness, generosity, moral courage, and the like. More than anything else, it is about how we treat other people."[49]
>
> DENNIS PRAGER

How do you become a good friend to others? Find people who inspire, encourage, and motivate you. Hang around them. Do everything you can to show that you are worthy of their friendship.

CHAPTER

Forgive Fast

atred breeds bitterness in your own heart. We can spend years holding a grudge against someone, only to discover that the other person never thought about the incident again … and that happens way more often than you think!

Don't let people live rent-free in your head.

If someone does you wrong, you can approach the person and try to reconcile. You can dissolve the relationship. You can forgive. Or you can drive yourself crazy with negative thoughts because you won't forgive.

True, the other person may be completely and totally in the wrong, and maybe they're not even the least bit sorry about it. And you know what? There is absolutely *nothing* you can do to change that.

We can only control ourselves, and it's time to let go of toxic people and move forward.

> "To forgive is to set a prisoner free and discover that the prisoner was you."[50]
> LEWIS B. SMEDES

Life is too short to hold on to frustrations. It's incredible how freeing it feels when you're finally able to forgive someone, no matter what wrong that person did to you.

That said, some things are truly despicable and terrible and can easily fit into the category of unforgivable. But it's *your* heart and emotions that will continue to hurt and grieve. Not theirs. In some circumstances, the best gift you can give yourself is the permission to talk to a counselor, therapist, parent, youth minister, pastor, or other trusted adult.

And how do you do know if you've forgiven someone?

> Author and pastor Rob Bell said it best in his Nooma video "Luggage," when he said you know you've forgiven someone when you can truly and honestly wish them well.[51]

what you
think about
all day long,
over long periods
eventually seeps
into your heart
as a belief.

GARY SMALLEY

garbage in, garbage out

i have often heard it said, "Garbage in, garbage out." The reality of how much our minds control our actions cannot be understated. In order to accomplish most anything in life, we must first win the battle in our minds. This is fought daily, and sometimes by the minute or hour. A positive mental attitude, a spirit of generosity and integrity, and purposeful determination are born in the mind first before they ever manifest into external actions. These things cannot be achieved short of feeding our minds the kind of information that should be consumed regularly. The habit of regularly consuming uplifting, informative, educational, and thoughtful content will benefit you greatly.

> "A man's mind may be likened to a garden, which may be intelligently cultivated or allowed to run wild; but whether cultivated or neglected, it must, and will, bring forth. If no useful seeds are put into it, then an abundance of useless weed seeds will fall therein and will continue to produce their kind."[52]
>
> JAMES ALLEN

Garbage out reflects in your speech, your actions, and in your goals and dreams.

Don't have goals or dreams?

Examine what you regularly fill your mind with.

Don't like how your actions affect others?

Assess those things you consume that are taking up residence in your mind and producing those behaviors.

Don't like what's coming out of your mouth, whether it's trashy or unkind, degrading or filthy?

It's time to take stock of what you allow into your brain. Fill it with beauty not garbage.

grit

> "Without effort, your talent is nothing more than unmet potential. Without effort, your skill is nothing more than what you could have done but didn't."[53]
>
> ANGELA DUCKWORTH

I f *hustle* had a twin, it would be *grit*—a characteristic of those who persevere through any obstacle that comes their way.

The overarching premise in Angela Duckworth's best-selling book *Grit* is that "as much as talent counts, efforts count twice."

Duckworth, the foremost leading expert on grit, studied multiple high achievers as part of her research on the subject.

What she found was fascinating. What really matters, more than how smart or how naturally talented and gifted you are, is the *effort you put forth*.

Did you try your best? Did you sufficiently prepare? Did you give it your all?

My brother-in-law says that he sleeps best at night when he knows that he's put forth a solid effort, made progress, and can put his head on his pillow, knowing he didn't waste a second. I think about this on the days when the most solid effort I made was getting off the couch to make something to eat. (After all, we all need a rest day sometimes!)

On the flip side, there should be a direct correlation between your effort and your results. Brilliance, intelligence, and intuition are all wonderful traits, and they will serve you well in life—but we must put in the work.

At the end of the day, when you lay your head on your pillow, it is my sincerest hope that you can be proud of the effort you contributed toward your goals and dreams. Don't ever let anyone knock you off that path and refuse to be intimidated by the kid who might be smarter than you.

Dig deep.

Work hard.

Persevere.

And watch as the doors fly open.

choose joy

D o you know someone who always seems to be happy? This person may not have everything they want or even need, but they are pleasant to hang around, and they somehow never fail to be full of joy.

This is the kind of person you should want to surround yourself with.

This is the type of person you should want to become.

You need to be aware of the personality you are developing. You have a choice to be intentional about the kind of person you will be—both now and in the future.

You can choose *joy* in the midst of the most challenging circumstances.

You can choose *happiness* in the midst of trial.

You can choose to be *content* with what you have.

You can choose to *encourage* others by using the time and resources you have.

Or, instead, you can choose to be moody, withdrawn, and ill tempered. As a matter of fact, if you want to fit in and be like every other teenager on the planet, go ahead and do just that.

But I think you want more out of life than that, don't you?

You aren't perfect, and I doubt you're saying that you lack room for improvement. What you are saying is that you are going to be aware that *you have the control!* You can choose to be joyful, even if your circumstances may not be.

> **"It is not joy that makes us grateful.
> It is gratitude that makes us joyful."[54]**
> ANONYMOUS

what
you aim at
determines
what you see.

JORDAN PETERSON

laugh at yourself

The trick to avoid extending an embarrassing situation is to laugh. It's also the quickest way to disarm future teasing.

Want to know how to avoid being laughed *at*?

Laugh together.

Kids smell weakness the same way sharks smell blood in the water miles away. We're all going to do embarrassing things. Accidents happen. Situations arise that can't be avoided.

It's how we handle those situations that determine the aftermath.

> "I learned that there's a certain character that
> can be built from embarrassing yourself

> endlessly. If you can sit happy with embarrassment, there's not much else that can really get to you."[55]
>
> CHRISTIAN BALE (the best Batman ever)

Let's say you trip in the lunchroom and half the school witnesses.

They're going to laugh. People always laugh when someone trips or drops something. Sometimes they clap, which is super embarrassing. Like, *can we not draw any more attention to the situation please?!*

So, how do you avoid getting teased or ending up with an unfortunate nickname?

Own it.

Trip? Take a bow.

Pass gas in class? Laugh it off.

Bask in the moment, for it is one that will pass quickly— as long as you show everyone watching that you are confident enough to handle it.

If you drop your head in shame, some mean kid will sense an opportunity. Don't give him the chance.

And if you witness another kid who falls prey to an embarrassing situation, be a friend, stand by them, and help them learn to laugh it off too.

CHAPTER **52**

World-changing kindness

> "Together we can change the world, just one random act of kindness at a time."[56]
>
> RON HALL

One of the things that is sorely missing from our society today is the quality of kindness. Unfortunately, in today's "cancel culture," it's more commonplace to cut someone off when we don't agree or if they make a mistake and say or do something dumb.

Instead of offering grace when others disagree with us or fail and disappoint us, it's far easier to just cut them out of our lives. It's unnatural to be a man of kindness.

Kindness is an attractive quality. Be a young man who is known for being kind—to the older adults in your life, your parents, classmates, friends, and even to complete strangers.

Because *that's* where the magic happens. When you give grace, you make an impact. Making an impact happens one small act of kindness at a time. You have no idea where that ripple of kindness might end up because you started it.

The book, *Same Kind of Different as Me*, gets me every time I read it. If you haven't read it yet, add it to your "to-read" list. It will change everything!

Here's a very poignant cut from one chapter that relates to kindness and how each of us can make a difference in someone's life:

> "You was the onlyest person that looked past my skin and past my meanness and saw that there was somebody on the inside worth savin ... We all has more in common than we think. You stood up with courage and faced me when I was dangerous, and it changed my life. You loved me for who I was on the inside, the person God meant for me to be, the one that had just gotten lost for a while on some ugly roads in life."[57]

By learning how to be kind, you will become an enjoyable employee, a friend that everyone can rely on—especially in the hard days. You will become known as a generous and giving spirit in a world that so desperately needs hope today.

Your kindness will literally be *world changing* if you allow it.

sit by the lonely kid

as Justin's younger brother headed out the door to go to one of his high school basketball games, his mother (my now mother-in-law) told him to be on the lookout for a kid who might be sitting alone that night.

I expected Josh, the captain of the basketball team, to brush her off, but instead he told her that he'd already reached out to him and would make sure the kid was included that night.

His response wasn't forced, nor was it the stereotypical, "Okay, Mom, sure, whatever you say," type of eye-roll response. And I was impressed, only because I had expected Josh to want to hang out with the other kids in his clique. But that just wasn't the case. This type of natural inclusivity made me want to become part of this family even more.

Because back in the day, I was that lonely kid. And I know how much it meant when someone paid attention or even acknowledged my existence.

> "Always try to leave people better than you found them ... Befriend the lost. Love the lonely."[58]
>
> AUTHOR UNKNOWN

Sometimes, it's the kids who are sitting by themselves that are the most loyal people you would ever hope to meet. There isn't a lot of competition for attention with them, so that means you can build a deep friendship relatively quickly.

You could also perhaps save a life.

A friend of mine has built a solid social media following by playing video games, and he told me that being kind to people he's playing with online has made a long-lasting impact. More than a couple of people told him they were on the verge of committing suicide before they connected with him.

A little kindness goes a long way.

And if you are the lonely kid, here's my advice: Take a deep breath, hold your head up high, and reach out to somebody. There's always another lonely kid, and he may just become your next best friend.

CHAPTER 54

be kind to those who can't help you

You probably know that, if you want favor at work, then it's important to be nice to your boss—but what about those who can't offer you anything? The way in which you treat those people speaks volumes about your character.

The next time you're at a restaurant, pay attention to how people treat the server. Is there someone who is rude to them? Who are the ones who say *thank you*? If a meal comes out and isn't quite right, how does the person handle it? This response can be valuable insider info into that person's heart.

The way we treat those who can't offer us a raise, new job, or do something amazing for us, is indicative of how we feel about people as a whole.

> **"I speak to everyone in the same way, whether he is the garbage man or the president of the university."**[59]
>
> ALBERT EINSTEIN

A friend of mine shared a story with me about a time when he had to wait in a hallway for a movie casting. He had acted in several films and was looking forward to this audition in particular. For whatever reason, and I don't have the specifics, it was taking way longer than normal.

Since the other actors in the waiting area weren't exactly being kind or friendly during this wait, my friend ended up chatting with a guy who worked in the building. And if memory serves, his position was janitor or something along that same level. Basically, he wasn't the guy who was making the casting decisions; because of that, he became the guy that everyone naturally ignored.

Anyway, my friend and this guy talked for a long time. It turns out this guy, even though he wasn't the decision-maker himself, was friends with the decision-maker. He pulled a couple strings and moved my friend up the audition line.

Guess who booked the role?

People often become so focused on the bigwigs that they sometimes mistreat those who have the bigwig's ear. This means that, even though the CEO might be the decision-maker, we should still ask—who does the CEO listen to?

The people who seemingly can't help you arrive at your preferred destination are sometimes *exactly* the people who can pave the way for you. And even if they are not, we have a moral obligation to treat people decently, no matter what their job title may be.

love others

It's pretty simple to love those who love us. People who are easy to love include friends and family, but it can also include strangers too—especially if they are kind, gentle, or treat us in a loving manner as well. Maybe they do something nice for us, smile when we are having a bad day, or offer encouragement when we need it.

But are we supposed to love those people we don't like? And what about those who are mean, or let's be honest, even evil? Should we still love them as well, or do we get a pass when people are difficult or different?

I would advise you now to understand that we should love others, regardless of what they can do for us, because the act of being loving will help you develop your character.

When you love others no matter what, you won't tolerate abuse of yourself or others; rather, you become known as someone who gives second chances, someone who helps where there's a need and shares with others for their benefit. Loving others is always the way to go. It is best to err on the side of love. At the end of the day, you can never love too much.

> "The only way to make sure you're happy is to love and care for others, even when they don't do the same. Spread love in the ways you know how, because the love you give is its own reward."[60]
>
> CONNOR CHALFANT

the ultimate
MEASURE OF A MAN
is not where he stands
in moments of
COMFORT
and convenience,
but where he stands
at times of
challenge
and controversy.

MARTIN LUTHER KING, JR

seek justice

here are major opportunities to practice justice today. On a daily basis, we each have the opportunity to be helpful to someone around us.

It could be a friend who is being bullied and needs just one person to stand up for them. You could be the one who makes a difference in someone's life just by standing by him or her. Because here's the truth: While you can't help *all* the people in the world, you can make a difference for at least one. If each person could do their part in eliminating injustice in the world, think of the difference that could make!

You could also help to tackle the larger problems in our society. Whether it's the struggle against racism, the issue of sex trafficking, or the fight for victims who have been abused in any way, the battle for justice is important. It's a big job—and that's why we need you.

> ## "Injustice anywhere is a threat to justice everywhere."[61]
> ### MARTIN LUTHER KING, JR.

Working for a purpose bigger than yourself is the key to living a happy and fulfilled life. I mean it. It is key to all the life decisions you will face ahead. You will live with both joy and peace if you seek to help others first rather than constantly striving to keep yourself comfortable.

Justice involves seeking to restore someone so they can enjoy the same opportunities you might have. You could fight for an entire people group, or even just one person. It doesn't matter. If you always seek to help others, you will never regret it. Living selflessly can't be beat. It's the opposite of what others might try to teach you. *Hustle hard, climb the ladder, get what you deserve*, they may say. Instead, I'm telling you the opposite: Treat others better than yourself and put them first. *This* is the best way to live your life!

are you the runner or the watcher?

hen a building catches on fire, some people run toward the chaos so they can help in any way possible. These people don't seem to care about their own safety. Others, however, pull their phones out and film from a distance.

Which person will you be? The runner or the watcher?

> "No one is useless in this world who lightens the burden of another."[62]
>
> CHARLES DICKENS

Not all tragedies are explosive. In fact, sometimes the deepest hurts are the ones that remain unspoken and unseen. Sometimes the crisis we need to run to is right in front of us.

We don't have to be fully equipped to be a listening ear or to be a strong shoulder for someone to lean on. Don't ever discount what you have to offer. When you find yourself in a similar situation, hurting and hoping someone will notice your need for help, you will be grateful for the people who step out of their comfort zones and run to you instead of sitting on the sidelines.

We don't have to be perfect in order to be productive.

> ### "To ease another's heartache is to forget one's own."[63]
> ABRAHAM LINCOLN, America's sixteenth president

It's not our job to fix everything, but it is our humanitarian obligation to help when we can.

CHAPTER

"what can i do?"

he key to building great relationships and to building success is to become others-focused and service-oriented.

When you do this, the question "What's in it for me?" becomes "What can I do for you?"

This will surprise and delight your parents, by the way. The next time you see your mom cleaning, ask her how you can help. If your dad is folding laundry, step in and take over.

Here's the big secret—and yes, this is a little self-serving, but it still works. The next time you want to be alone to play a game, read, or anything along those lines, instead ask your parents what you can do for them *first*. Give them the opportunity to dole out a couple of chores.

Once you have helped your parents—or maybe they have excused you from working—you are then granted the freedom to have alone time. This can be a relief for you, because it gives you a chance to enjoy your free time without worrying that your parents will pop into your bedroom and command that you take the trash out.

Also, if you have siblings, this will give your parents a chance to see that you are more helpful than they are. Because of that, the next chores might go to your siblings.

Those are selfish motivations, yes, but they often work. The bigger picture here is this: Get into the habit of asking what you can do for others before you think about yourself.

> **"Always render more and better service than is expected of you, no matter what your task may be."[64]**
>
> OG MANDINO, author of *The Greatest Salesman in the World*

Habits that you build in your teens will be carried into your adult years. Imagine how much more valuable you can be to a company when you ask how you can help instead of constantly watching the clock, waiting for your break time and the weekend to arrive.

This character trait will also serve you well if you go into business for yourself. People love to be part of something bigger than them, and if your mission is focused on others first, then you've got yourself a win-win scenario.

The people I know who are always helping others rarely ask for help themselves. However, if there ever came an opportunity for me to help them out, I would drop everything to do so. We shouldn't do good deeds for others purely for the sake of getting something in return, but it is still a positive consequence of being others focused.

So the next time you have an opportunity to do so, ask someone, "Hey, is there anything I can do for you?" and then enjoy the rewards that come from helping others.

CHAPTER

get wisdom

I t's sometimes easy to confuse knowledge with wisdom, and it's hard to explain what the difference is to others. Over the years, I have recognized the difference: Knowledge covers facts. This entails the things you can study and learn. We can all gain knowledge. Information is literally available at our fingertips at all times.

> "Knowledge is knowing what to say.
> Wisdom is knowing when to say it."[65]
>
> ANONYMOUS

But wisdom has a little different connotation. To me, the biggest difference is that wisdom implies that knowledge already exists, but it's taken to the next level. Wisdom involves *actual application* of the knowledge!

Wisdom is evident in our decisions to avoid spending this week's paycheck on snacks, video game upgrades, or other frivolous items. Instead, we use the money to save for the car we want, the gas we need, or the date we want to go on. When we choose to work instead of play, to do our school-work instead of scroll through social media—or when we refrain from doing the dangerous trick that would risk physical harm—each of those decisions are rooted in wisdom!

Demonstrating wisdom is a sign of maturity. The more we practice it, the easier it becomes, and then we can grow all the wiser!

in matters of style
**swim with
the current;**
in matters of principle,
**stand like
a rock.**

THOMAS JEFFERSON

CHAPTER **60**

ON VALUES
AND WORLDVIEW

> "The ultimate measure of a man is not where he stands in moments of comfort and convenience, but where he stands at times of challenge and controversy."[66]
>
> MARTIN LUTHER KING, JR.

olding the right values begins with staying rooted in honesty. This requires being intentional about telling the truth in both the small and the big things of life. Eliminate little white lies and keep your word to others. By being a man of your word, you prove that you value others.

Your entire worldview affects your values. If you are only consumed with yourself—your own desires, needs, and happiness—then you will be very disappointed and lonely when you reach the end of your life. A life spent in sacrifice and service to others will matter far more than all the money, houses, or material gain you can accumulate.

Being a man who doesn't value others, on the other hand, will create a deficit to those around you. Others will discern when you are lacking integrity or honesty, and they will not value you in return.

Your values shape your destiny. If you don't value honesty and integrity, then that will be lacking from your life. If you don't value life, liberty, and the pursuit of happiness, then you will soon realize it's missing from your life. If you don't value the friends and family you have, don't worry, they will know it and will remove themselves from your life.

Try to develop a healthy worldview with both intentionality and purpose. Be a man who values moral integrity and observe how people will value you in return. Learn how to treat others the way you would like to be treated. It won't be perfect, but often these values will be mirrored back to you in return.

ENDNOTES

1 https://peacealliance.org/tools-education/peace-inspirational-quotes/
2 https://www.successories.com/iquote/category/3/anger-quotes/1
3 https://www.brainyquote.com/authors/peter-blair-henry-quotes
4 Some sites have this quote attributed as "unknown" but Goodreads attributes it to Mark Matthews, thus the credit given. https://www.goodreads.com/author/quotes/7363031.Mark_Matthews | Accessed April 27, 2021.
5 https://www.thepositivemom.com/35-powerful-quotes-that-will-make-you-rethink-gossip
6 https://www.quotesweekly.com/motivational-quotes-on-laziness-to-overcome-it/
7 https://www.azquotes.com/quote/1269116
8 https://www.brainyquote.com/authors/frederick-william-faber-quotes
9 https://www.brainyquote.com/topics/lust-quotes
10 https://www.azquotes.com/quote/666797
11 https://quotefancy.com/quote/879398/Oprah-Winfrey-Don-t-settle-for-a-relationship-that-won-t-let-you-be-yourself
12 https://www.goodreads.com/quotes/860053-don-t-let-feeling-lonely-push-you-into-the-arms-of
13 https://www.brainyquote.com/quotes/mark_twain_414009
14 https://www.awakenthegreatnesswithin.com/35-inspirational-quotes-on-priorities/
15 https://www.businessinsider.com/personal-finance/good-habits-of-self-made-millionaires#2-they-exercise-2

16 https://www.businessinsider.com/personal-finance/
good-habits-of-self-made-millionaires#2-they-exercise-2

17 https://wisdomquotes.com/inspirational-quotes-for-men/

18 https://www.awakenthegreatnesswithin.com/35-inspirational-quotes-
on-preparation/

19 https://www.wow4u.com/balancequotes/

20 https://www.azquotes.com/quote/356417

21 https://www.growthengineering.co.uk/55-quotes-about-learning/

22 https://www.goodreads.com/quotes/tag/perception

23 https://quotessayings.net/topics/participation-trophies/

24 https://www.stlouisfed.org/education/economic-lowdown-video-series/no-
such-thing-free-lunch

25 https://books.google.com/books?id=nqd9DwAAQBAJ&pg=PA143&lpg=
PA143&dq="Never+spend+your+money+before+you+earned+it."+Thomas+
Jefferson&source=bl&ots=piZIN5wiAX&sig=ACfU3U0qBtqc9-_
AxyRYvqQ9Poh-PbyBVg&hl=en&sa=X&ved=2ahUKEwjr-
87g2NTwAhVUF1kFHRtGA2MQ6AEwEHoECBUQAw#v=onepage&q=
"Never%20spend%20your%20money%20before%20you%20earned%20it."
%20Thomas%20Jefferson&f=false

26 https://wisdomquotes.com/inspirational-quotes-for-men/

27 https://www.azquotes.com/author/2136-Warren_Buffett/tag/integrity

28 https://www.sun-sentinel.com/features/sfl-flstory--chinaflowernbaug28-
story.html

29 https://www.brainyquote.com/quotes/rick_warren_395865?src=t_humility

30 https://www.inc.com/dave-kerpen/15-quotes-that-remind-us-of-the-
awesome-power-of-humility.html

31 https://createmytherapistwebsite.com/grow-your-practice-asking-help/

32 https://www.brainyquote.com/topics/brave-man-quotes

33 https://www.azquotes.com/quote/1385867

34 https://www.successories.com/iquote/category/883/diligence-quotes/1

35 https://www.brainyquote.com/quotes/leo_tolstoy_121890

36 https://www.awakenthegreatnesswithin.com/35-inspirational-quotes-
on-honesty/

37 http://quotetab.com/quote/by-james-e-faust/when-we-tell-little-white-
lies-we-become-progressively-color-blind-it-is-better?source=remain

38 https://www.wow4u.com/truthquotes/

39 https://www.forbes.com/sites/kevinkruse/2012/10/16/quotes-on-
leadership/?sh=34b41de22feb

40 https://www.goodreads.com/author/quotes/12008.Peter_F_Drucker

41 https://www.goodreads.com/quotes/34863-the-heights-by-great-men-
reached-and-kept-were-not

42 https://stevemaraboli.net/aboutsteve/

43 https://inspiration.rightattitudes.com/authors/albert-camus/

44 https://wisdomquotes.com/respect-quotes/

45 https://www.searchquotes.com/quotes/about/Correction/#ixzz6qsZEshcu

46 https://www.goodreads.com/quotes/8692448-too-many-men-i-know-
experience-shame-because-society-places

47 https://greatpeopleinside.com/nonverbal-communication-part1/

48 https://www.positivityblog.com/friendship-quotes/

49 https://www.brainyquote.com/quotes/dennis_prager_471259
50 https://www.brainyquote.com/quotes/lewis_b_smedes_135524
51 https://www.firstlutherancr.org/renovare-blog/week-6-nooma-luggage-rob-bell
52 https://www.goodreads.com/author/quotes/8446.James_Allen
53 https://www.goodreads.com/work/quotes/45670634-grit-passion-perseverance-and-the-science-of-success
54 https://savingjoyfully.com/my-top-20-favorite-quotes-on-joy-why-i-choose-joy/
55 https://www.gas-x.com/amp/quotes-embarrassing-situation.html
56 https://www.brainyquote.com/authors/ron-hall-quotes
57 https://www.goodreads.com/work/quotes/421493-same-kind-of-different-as-me
58 https://tinybuddha.com/wisdom-quotes/always-try-leave-people-better-found-hug-hurt-kiss-broken-befriend-lost-love-lonely/
59 https://www.goodreads.com/quotes/3972-i-speak-to-everyone-in-the-same-way-whether-he
60 https://www.goodreads.com/quotes/tag/loving-others
61 https://www.birthdaywishes.expert/quotes-about-justice/
62 https://sermonquotes.com/sermonquotes/6550-no-one-is-useless.html
63 https://www.goodreads.com/quotes/203743-to-ease-another-s-heartache-is-to-forget-one-s-own
64 https://www.brainyquote.com/quotes/og_mandino_157862
65 https://www.awakenthegreatnesswithin.com/35-inspirational-quotes-on-wisdom/
66 https://wisdomquotes.com/inspirational-quotes-for-men/

RESOURCES

BOYS TOWN NATIONAL HOTLINE:

1-800-448-3000

DATING VIOLENCE? TEEN PEER ADVOCATES:

1-800-331-9474   ·   *LoveIsRespect.org*

THINKING ABOUT RUNNING AWAY?

1-800-RUNAWAY

DAY ONE HOTLINE (LEARN THE TELL-TALE SIGNS OF ABUSIVE RELATIONSHIPS):

1-866-223-1111   ·   *DayOneServices.org*

CRISIS TEXT LINE:

Free 24/7 support—text 741741 · *CrisisTextLine.org*

NATIONAL DOMESTIC VIOLENCE HOTLINE:

1-800-799-7233 (SAFE) · *TheHotline.org*

DEPRESSED, OVERWHELMED, OR SUICIDAL? NATIONAL SUICIDE PREVENTION LIFELINE:

1-800-273-TALK